LASSETER'S DIARY

Transcribed with Mud-Maps

Compiled and transcribed by Tom Thompson

ETT IMPRINT
Exile Bay

This edition published by ETT Imprint, Exile Bay 2024

First facsimile edition published 1986 by Angus & Robertson
First published by ETT Imprint 2020.

Compiled and transcribed by Tom Thompson

ETT IMPRINT

PO Box R1906

Royal Exchange NSW 1225

Australia

ISBN 978-1-923024-84-7 (paper)
ISBN 978-0-925416-01-0 (ebook)

Cover: Lasseter's tree, carved by Walter Gill on June 1931, to denote where Lasseter's body was found, incised thus:
LASSITER.
Died.
Jan 1931.

Designed by Tom Thompson

Preface

Harold Bell Lasseter claimed in 1929 to have previously found a fabulous reef of gold in Central Australia and managed to convince a group of investors to find the treasure. The Central Australian Gold Expedition (C.A.G.E.) company was formed, to be led by veteran bushman Fred Blakeley. It was beset with disagreement and high drama, and Lasseter was left alone in the desert, where he died in early 1931. A further expedition that year was mounted by Bob Buck, and Lasseter was found, along with his buried diary.

Ion Idriess engaged with this expedition, and purchased the diary from Lasseter's widow, transcribing much of it in his bestseller, Lasseter's Last Ride (Angus & Robertson 1931). For purposes of story-telling, Idriess presented sections not in the diary order, and intriguingly, offered up two further mud-maps in this book (pages 85 and 86 herein). The diary then formed part of the A & R Archive sold to the State Library of New South Wales in 1977, where it can be found in the Mitchell Library: MLMMS 3269.

Angus & Robertson published a facsimile edition of the diary in June 1986. This transcription was aided by sighting the original diary, the facsimile and checking Idriess's own account. Lasseter's mud-maps on page 40 take up three pages in the diary, on page 41 (two pages) and on page 42 (two pages), and these variants, as published in 1931, are clearer than those in the battered diary. The map on page 80 was published in 1931, and is complete, unlike the diary or facsimile pages. Good hunting!

Tom Thompson
Exile Bay, NSW

Cave culpee
stone bully
dirt munda
tree caroo
man wattee
woman lubra
child piccaninny (small)
spear wero
wood becky
fire werro
stick bunna
hill ditto
creek ditto
water caapee
beard nannygoat
foot kinna

hand malla or gryah
arm ninna
leg alpa or colpa capa
body wela
head mala
hair catta
eye curro
nose milla
teeth cattee
pigeon tulba
emu calaah
[indecipherable] malu
basin wera or weda
[indecipherable] peka

12345678910
11 12
ABCDEFGHIJ
KLMNOPQR
STUVWXYZ
JIM
PIGEON

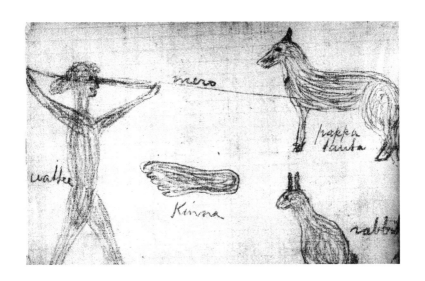

Old fellow returned with despatch book today Larry failed to get thro' to Alice Springs. He was all played out so I gave him a rabbit I had dug out.

Later in the day the black who had just raided my camp showed up & told the tribe that I had tried to shoot him & I had only turned in about an hour when 20 of them came down, woke me up, and told me they were going to

The C.A.G.E. 1930 expedition members (left to right): Coote, Sutherland, Colson, Blakeley, Taylor and Lasseter at front.

kill me. The headman who is so treacherous being the leader & spokesman I succeeded in bluffing them by talking a lot & refusing to get up I told them how I had engaged him to show me the way South for 3 days & how he had raided me the first day & they postponed the killing till tomorrow (he heard me yell "I'll shoot")

As soon as I was assured they had retired I rose & made a moonlight flit for 5 miles back to the cave again. (the old fellow had moved my camp for me to where rabbits were more plentiful) now that tomorrow is here and they find I have moved I expect an attack in force tonight. In the dust of the cave I have just unearthed an unexpected find 5 revolver cartridges. Tho' as they know I am practically blind that may not avail me much two or more spears were carried by each man. No doubt they were in deadly earnest too, so I don't suppose I've an earthly chance of surviving I can carry 2 gallons & 3 pints of water but that is hardly likely to take me the 80 miles to Mt Olga & on no food whatever I've brought this all on myself by going alone but I thought the blacks, tho' primitive were fair dealing.

Goodbye & Gold Bless you Rene darling wife of mine & may God Bless the children

I would shoot a blackfellow & told me to get up & be speared *currotta* whatever that word means and they were in deadly earnest too.

I flatly refused to get up & finally persuaded them to postpone the killing till today as soon as I was assured they had retired I made a moonlight flit back to the cave. The old chap I have mentioned had moved me 5 miles – here I am established with plenty of water but no food and as I am cut off from supplies

I see my finish as soon as they raise the rest of the tribe to rush the cave, they can stand on top & spear me as I come near the entrance anyway. I had an unexpected find of 5 revolver cartridges & hope I can made every shot tell. The young headman I have previously mentioned was leader & spokesman of the party. Of course I am myself to blame for tackling this job alone, but I thought I could trust the blacks

not to do anything worse than raid me. Good Bye Rene
darling wife of mine & don't grieve remember you must
live for the children now dear, but it does seem cruel to die
alone out here because I have been too good to the blacks
my last prayer is "God be merciful to me, as sinner & be
good to those I leave behind

XXX Harry X

yesterday the old man returned with the despatch book having failed to get thro' to Alice Spgs. Later in the day the chap who first raided showed up at the camp & told them I had said I would shoot him" (I yelled that I would shoot when I say him getting away with the gear & he heard me but knew he was out of range) so last night I got a most unpleasant surprise I had been asleep for an hour or so, when a party 20 strong came down suddenly, woke me up & told me they were going to kill me for saying

Blacks tried to kill me today while I was waiting for a rabbit three spears were thrown but two shots drove them off one spear landed in the tree I had my back against within 3 inches of my neck the other two were on the side they have sneaked in the whole tribe I saw three big smoke & noticed a lot of blacks moving in the

On the trail, the C.A.G.E. expedition 1930.

why am I abandoned like this Paul Johns should have showed up with tucker 6 weeks ago. He gave me his word of Honor. Blakely assured me relief would be sent if I had not returned 1st November, it is now in January but I have lost count of dates I think about 16th or 18th. 5 cwt tucker Ilbilla & me starving here. Why have not the people organised a relief

This agony is awful 4 plums in three days. Why is no relief sent what became of Paul. The suspense of not knowing is the worst of all. Why do I cling so to life when a shot would end my torment its just because I want to know why everyone has failed me. To die a lonely horrible death is bad, but not to know why is worse it is now 25 days since the camels bolted allowing 10 days to Ilbilba they should be near home by now, then people will speculate a week as to where I am, then someone will be sent to Ilbilba a black probably who will loiter on the way then too late camels will be despatched over my route 360 miles via Ilbilba & a motor truck could get to me in two days if they

Camels on the C.A.G.E. expedition

only knew I am at Winters Glen, a light car would do it in one. Oh, my God its awful. How I long to see my children once more to hold their chubby hands & to see their laughing faces & hear their baby prattle My God why does not help come, with lots of water I can hold out for several days yet but the agony of starvation

may drive me to shoot myself. I think it the worst possible
death with one experience of this country I should never
have gone alone but I relied on Paul to follow me what good
a reef worth millions I would give it all for a loaf of bread and
to think that only a week away is lots of tucker the blacks are
not troubling me now they know I am dying and will wait

I erred in treating the natives too kindly Paul was right in saying you must treat them rough they are born thieves & steal the most essential things tucker & the means of getting it

I am paying the penalty with my life may it be a lesson to others

Lasseter

even then I might have won out on 3 lb rice were it not for the Sandy blight blinding me till I was unable to follow tracks. I suppose the plans I buried under camp fire are blistered & useless with this heat. I ought to have buried them in this cave.

I find that these blacks are the most treacherous people on earth, there is one here, a young headman, who understands a smattering of English. He posed as my friend and I gave him my remaining blanket & billy & sheath knife, and what remained of the tent peg then he introduced a young lubra into my camp and I put her out once, but he brought her again so I gave her my watch & a clean handkerchief & cake of soap & sent her back to camp then he had 16 men with 2 spears each bar my path to a rabbit burrow up creek I took a risk & unloaded my revolver ostentatiously I had only 3 live cartridges in it anyway then folded my arms & walked right up & thro' the cordon then went & camped at his camp fire body touching body & slept the night thro'

Next morning I got up

early & went to see if I had snared any rabbits & I caught one so sat down & cooked & ate it, to find when I got back to camp that I had been raided again even a spoon & razor being found & stolen this headman wears a white hair hand & has white penis apron or fringe.

Later an old chap with a wart 6 inches by 3 inches in the fold of his posteria took pity on me & brought 2 rabbits & some berries like cape gooseberries, my

Old Warts, who befriended Lasseter.

eyes are still blurry & smart a good deal but are much better than last week. To my way of thinking this is the ninth day after the camels bolted & I hear they went north (Ilbilla way) so may reach the Mission in a couple of months

Too late to benefit me. I may as well write finish to my life chapter it is only will power that is holding me up, & that is dam poor sustenance

If my feet were only tough but the irony of it is, that my feet are the tenderest part of my body. I leave my everlasting curse on Blakely & Jenkins, Blakely for not sending the relief as promised and Jenkins for omitting the Argerol

Darling I want you to remember me as when we first met & not the scarecrow that I now am have shrunk still further & the flies & ants have nearly eaten my face

I can do nothing against them "beaten by Sandy Blight" what an epitaph, I keep one hand constantly swishing while I am awake but it just serves to knock a hole thro' the swarm & they work day & night

Oh Rene what a fool I was to rely on promises to send relief. I don't know for sure what happened to Paul Johns but I left him within reach of civilization & he

Albert Paul Johns, dingo hunter, was the last man to see Lasseter, leaving him near Ilibilba in late October 1930

understood & could talk the language fluently. I had one of
the young men all day trying to teach him but they are so
dense

I tried most of the day to learn his language but when I
would point to anything & try to find out what it was the
answer was usually a repetition of my word. I tried one day
to teach a piccaninny the numerals on a watch dial & he got
so he could point to them & repeat them, then

two old men dropped in & said something to him & he turned into a block of wood for density. I wonder if the old men knew I was trying to educate him & objected.

Poisoned

Today. I crept out to try & get some green feed and chewed a herb which was poison.

Old man with wart very kind.

Young blacks gathered round & laughed.

Fired my 3 shots & they ran like hell paroxisms passed but

too weak to move

Love Harry

After all Im not dead yet but I thought I was a goner. Yesterday as a final flutter I drank the remaining brandy, half bottle of castor oil & the last Seidlitz powder. I suppose the combination of all three effected the cure, but Im still very weak. The old man came again with a rabbit & three young parrots. Very acceptable then the irony of it is about ½ dozen others crop in and help to eat & they eat the biggest share. I stewed the rabbit &

got the gravy anyway.

Ive tried to amuse the blacks by drawing pictures but somehow they don't appeal. I am as helpless as a kitten now & they know it. I was turned adrift this morning & told to shift for myself. The young buck that introduced the lubra being very arrogant tho' I gave him this blanket camp sheet tommyhawk & sheath knife. The old chap I have

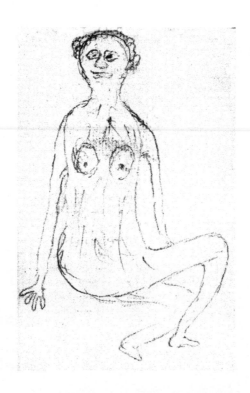

previously mentioned with the long beard & wart took pity
on my to the extent of carrying my things 5 miles up stream
where more water was available & built me a bough shelter
alongside it juts where Paul & I had the job with the camels
bogging. I have 2 snares left but the blacks have been 100
strong

on the creek all the week & have pretty near got every rabbit.
They cannot get enough for themselves now I suppose is the
reason they turned me adrift. I have told him he can have
everything I leave behind if he gets this book to Alice Springs.

I suppose it is neat & proper that I should say
"God have mercy on me & be good to those I leave behind"

Harry

I have watched & hoped for relief till I am about the end of my tether & am in very bad shape indeed. The 5 mile walk was simply awful for me tho the old fellow carried the pack Tucker is the one & only necessity here

Oddly enough the two prospecting pans that were stolen were returned to me by the young headman today but he retained the presents I had given him.

Lasseter with supply truck, C.A.G.E expedition 1930.

The lubra that he introduced to me was named Angola he said the word about 100 times to impress me with it but when I tried to find out his name he simply repeated all I said.

Dearest Rene I am sorry to finish out here & the worry of not knowing how you are faring & knowing how you must be in suspense as to my fate is simply the worst pain of all. Teach the children to believe the best you can of their father and soften the tale of my suffering here. If I could only know what the trouble is all about that no relief was sent or anything done at all. Oh it is awful indeed and the skeleton of me can scarce support the weight of my clothes. Im an awful sight & the flies are maddening & ants something that Hell can not improve on

The blacks must have seen me burying stuff on the sandhill

for they brought in the films that I had buried under the fire so I have now buried them under the floor of cave top end.

I scratched the hole out last night when I feel sure they were not about but oh what does it matter. I want relief & have saved one cartridge but will stick it out as long as possible

The old man has just come & pointed the water & bough shelter out to me again saying *capei caro capei caro* about 1 dozen times

I am giving him this book & saying

Alice Springs,
Alice Springs, 100 times

Kindest regards to all dear & kiss mother for me

I loved you always as I love you now with all my heart &

soul. "God be good to me a sinner"

AMEN

Ayers Rock

E
X
S

Mr Olga

Sandhills & mulga

S

Breakaways

Difficult country

S
Near lake
Scattered mulga gums and oak

Lake Amadeus

Bog hole

Sandhills Camp
Mulga S desert oaks
Patches of big gums

Sandhills
and
big
breakaways

and oaks

Gums—some 70 ft.
high

Camp

S

Rough
very
vegetation

Country
scrubby

breakaways

S

Camp

S

Sandhills
limestone
with
ironstone

scrubby

Camp

Gravel
beds
Mallee

41

Camp

Mallee
dense mulga
S
Petarde
Spring

Camp

Small
saltbush
plain

E
X
N

Noon

Sandhills &
oak

Pharaohs
head

m͏ʳ
Tudor

Outline
of
Childs head
290 ft. high

Camp

Sandhills
and
oak

E
X
N

M͏ᶜ
Tudor
west

Pers   Pass camp

Pasar' Pass

LOW BLUFF HILLS

Potardi ← 50 M · Camp

S
E

noon C

S
×
E

⊕ camp

denne mulga   Bailey Ridge

S

Quartz
outcrops   more

                  dense

                       mulga

S

            camp

                  Sandhills

                     &

                  Scattered
                       mulga

Ubilla ⊕

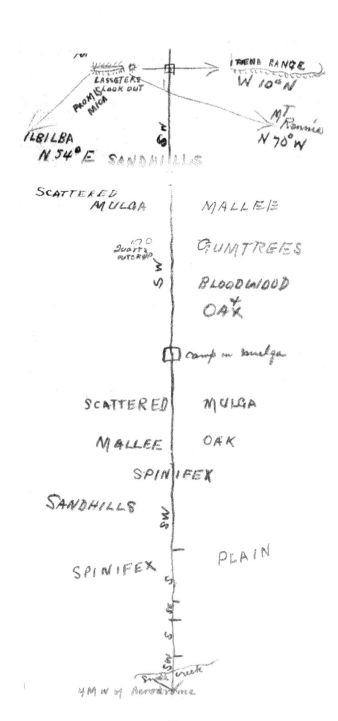

TOR

LASSETERS
PROMIS LOOK OUT
MICA

TREND RANGE
W 10° N

MT Rennie
N 70° W

ILBILBA
N 54° E SANDHILLS

SCATTERED
MULGA
MALLEE

GUMTREES

Quartz
outcrop
BLOODWOOD

OAK

camp in mulga

SCATTERED
MULGA

MALLEE
OAK

SPINIFEX

SANDHILLS

PLAIN

SPINIFEX

Small creek
4 M W of Aerodrome

45

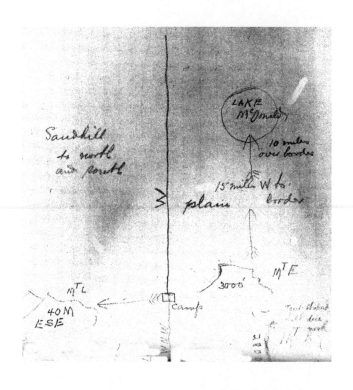

Spinifex

Mulga

Mallee

Interspersed on this plain

small 400ft hill

N×N

Sandhill

country

scrubs

Spinifex   and Mulga

sandhills × dying out
Mallee   Scattered lemmora

noon☐camp

Spinifex

                        and

Sandhills × with desert Oak

camp Small rock outcrops
Spinifex   plain

                    Rocky Pinnacle
        mulga + Spinifex
Sandal   between Sandhills
off here
going SW

M' Brown
S 25° W

Mulba aerodrome

Small ironstone
outcrop where truck
caught fire

Camp

Orange Sandhill
base

N 60 W

noon

Sandhill
&
Mulga

Sandhills

N 52 W

Camp

Sandhills
&
Mulga

W 18° N

rotten granite
outcrops
red soil

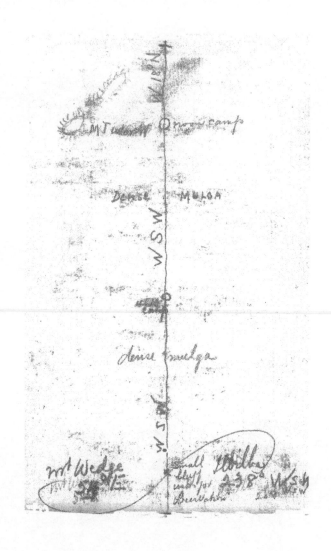

Too/o/oo "17 creek
Warren   cone Shaped hill
4 M East [ ] 10M due N
mulga +   Spinifex

>3M camp

Gorge with Permanent
Water on Nside

L E I B I G   dry sandy creek
do   15M Gilbra to west

mulga

ikely water obtainable creek about 15ft dry sandy
by shallow   8M bed approach to W
MT   excav   and
LEIBIG   Spinifex

TAYLOR'S creek
                3M Well of laurus

Dear Rene

I think I am near my finish I am nearly blind & crazy with Sandy blight tormented with flies & ants.
As a last recourse I soused my eyes in Lourdes Water last night & they are much clearer today but I am so weak from lack of [indecipherable] I can hardly walk. I used precious cartridges [indecipherable] shoot just [indecipherable] of skim milk running out of my

eyes all the time and I can't see [indecipherable] straight I am [indecipherable] cartridges am at [indecipherable] there is [indecipherable] I tried out East but [apparently?] went up a glen to where I expected to find a rockhole with 100 gals water but there was only a cupful & when I got back to where I had hung the flour bag in a tree blacks had raided me to [indecipherable] ounce. I have about 3 lbs rice & am making rice cakes

I feel sure it is the same family of blacks (five of them) that is/
are stalking (me?)
I examined the tracks for over an hour and am sure they are
the same, I am now in a cave at the glen and have only about
20 [indecipherable] to go for Water,
[indecipherable] me the blacks have (not?) molested me yet
but [indecipherable] member [indecipherable] about
[indecipherable] one [indecipherable] there is a
[indecipherable] of some

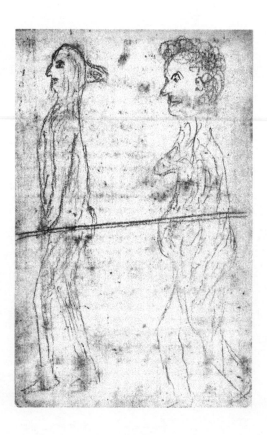

kind going on [indecipherable] in the [camp?
indecipherable] try and get [indecipherable] 11 snares
[indecipherable] three more [kangaroos?] the blacks
[indecipherable] my way to the rabbits
I was hopeful that the camels might come in to water but
they have evidently wandered towards Ilbilba so that if they
do return to Alice Springs it will be 2 months before [they?]
get there & then it will be too late for a rescue party

I've done my best darling & am sure I could have got out of it had not been for this Sandy blight I tried it hard to forgive Jack Jenkin for his wilful neglect there I put it in writing & urged upon him the necessity of including [an?] ounce or two in the medicine chest but he put [indecipherable] instead [indecipherable] does not cure, the flies

torment me night & day I wast [ed hours?] for an
[indecipherable] yesterday [indecipherable] the
[indecipherable] rissen from [indecipherable] keep spit on
my fingers & rubbing [my own?] eyes to keep them open &
now they smart & burn, its awful.

Darling I've pegged the reef & marked the exact locality on
the map which is buried in my kit [indecipherable] on the
Sand hill where the Camels bolted – on the East Side of Hill.

and I photographed [datum?] peg dated 23 Dec.

I cant understand [why?] support or relief has not been afforded me. I wrote Edward & also asked Carrington the Govt. Resident, to send word to the Company to send me [indecipherable] they did not [indecipherable] one with a consolidated miners right but expected [indecipherable] to p [indecipherable] square [indecipherable] 28 acre [indecipherable] 5 pegs to a block & 8 trenches just figure out the amount of work necessary there would be 120 [indecipherable] a [indecipherable] work for [review?]

I made myself some rabbit sox dear you would laugh at me in them but they are easy on my feet.

I buried 3 rolls of film in a 5 lb treacle tin on the sandhill too there are some interesting photos there of one of a family of seven [indecipherable] you will understand why I took a side View.

then there is a photo of a water hole, it is on [the?] West Australian border .

I had a swim in it just lovely, it is 150 ft long and 22 ft wide over half its length and over 24 ft deep at the other end which [indecipherable] to 15 ft.

Im so [indecipherable] the diary I kept of this last trip of mine is [indecipherable] interest [indecipherable] read.

Towing across central Australia and

sometimes they leaned heavy on the tow line

I am [hiding?] this [under a] rock in the
[indecipherable] of [indecipherable] but of course you will
know that if it is found.

A bunch [of wild?] pigeons have just flown up from the
Water hole so I know the blacks are round somewhere the
pigeons make such a whirr with their wings.

Darling there is such a lot I would like to say to you but I
can't write it where anyone might [see?]

I've tried to make you happy & if the Company treat you right you will be rich the reef is a bonanza & to think that if only Fred Blakely had been guided by me we could have got there with the truck in three [weeks?] damnable that man should be caricatured by the most satirical in Sydney his [pretty?] ambition is to feed from woman's breast. he wants

A camel's view of the 1930 C.A.G.E. expedition.

six wetnurses each guaranteed to give a quart at a milking
I would suggest [that] Smiths Weekly satirize him by
[showing] him surrounded by wetnurses
[indecipherable] him & fighting for the privilege of putting
diapers on him

I would suggest that as personal equipment for him as
leader of a gold seeking expedition he be furnished with 24
dozen diapers tablecloth size and a guard of Wetnurses

Give my love to the children & may we meet again.

Darling I have always believed in a God, a super ruler of the universe, but I have gone my own way so long that Im ashamed to pray to Him now

I know [indecipherable] "Call upon me in the time of trouble & I will deliver thee" but my ideas of time of trouble & his may not coincide. I have taken up 10 holes in my waist belt & still it is loose so you can see how I have fallen away

Im just a skeleton now and I always thought (well) of the blacks till now

only 2 weeks ago or less I made them some beautiful rabbit pies now they are waiting for me to die in order to steal my shirt & trousers off the body.

I suppose the Children have grown immensely since I saw them last

Joy may not remember me but the others will

How I would love to see them once more, to romp on the [couch?] with them & to have their chubby arms round me

Of course I was a fool to take this on alone but I relied on Paul Johns overtaking me in 4 to 6 weeks at the outside. He averred that he would overtake me in three weeks & gave his word of Honor not to let me down.

Also it was agreed upon Fred Blakely when I

engaged to go with the camels that if I did not show up again by the end of November that they would send a man named Johansen to my relief. As I believe he also stumbled on to this identical reef I had to go right out to Lake Christopher which is 100 miles across the WA border in order to get my bearings then I was going to go direct to the reef. The Company was foolish mixing up politics with it all because A Blakeley was Minister for Home & Tim & Fred was Ambitious have the road across Central Australia named "Blakely Highway." the monstrous conceit of the man. He never did a thing to deserve such a memorial. A[nd if he] had not revised [our?] food supplies & cure all the fresh meat & fish

I would have been able to get along nicely. I have 6 tins of corned [beef?] now but I simply [can't?] touch them

We had 750 lbs corned beef 6 Hams (Very salt) & 3 doz tins of kipper snacks smallest size & also very salt. I wanted a case of sardines but Blakely cut it out. Curse the man may he be fed on corned beef [alone?]

I have just measured my chest I have shrunk from 35 to 29 inches.

Lasseter finalising the supplies for the 1930 C.A.G.E. expedition.

and my waist line has an even greater shrinkage I don't know
whether to record it as a miracle [or?] not but my eyes seem
a lot easier since I soused them with Lourdes Water
yesterday and last night I was able to get a rabbit tho' it cost
me three cartridges

I would try & make it to Mt Olga if I only [indecipherable] of
but one waterhole [between] but 80 miles is a long stretch
with no water

nor food nor am I sure of meeting with friendly blacks who
would give me a feed. I saw [five?] tracks this morning it
was the same family which raided me, that scared the
pigeons yesterday

they sneak about in the rocks above this cave

I cant see them but the birds scare out of a ti-tree that grows
(only) once in awhile. I feel inclined to shoot one

so you can see my feelings have suggested great change.

It may interest you & others to know that in my opinion the whole of the Area I have traversed, - 200 x 300 miles, is based on one vast bed of limestone that shows evidence of having been burned & therefore acts like sponge & absorb the water which falls.

The water get away

from the surface so fast that 3 inches which fell in 20 minutes at Lake Chris[topher] at 3.30 to 3.50 PM [indecipherable] which I measured in a 6 quart billy set on top of an 8 gallon drum) was all gone in an hour with the exception of a few puddles in the Lake.

Evaporation could not account for all that, so it must soak into the soil & as the lake is quite close [indecipherable] I figure the lime [indecipherable] absorb it and [indecipherable] for a long time

My opinion is [plenty?] of shafts about
[indecipherable] sunk about 20 feet [into?] rock would
furnish a permanent water supply for a limited number of
people and cattle and there is amount of feed for cattle
especially below Lake Amadeus.

The rabbits have been numerous but were thinned out by
[indecipherable] but they are beginning [to come?] up again.
I have seen [them?] from Mt Olga to Lake Christopher, they
are thickest in the

Petersman range, likewise the dingo. My eyes seem to be easing the smart quite [well?] but the flies are trou[blesome?]

Mrs Obrien will be pleased to think that the Lourdes Water helped me, and Im sure it did. Give them my Very Kindest regards, dear, they were friends indeed.

This morning I had a visit from another
[tribe?] of blacks who [indecipherable] Camels making [indecipherable] North, so Im [indecipherable]

will make for [indecipherable] & thence to the
[indecipherable] & may reach [indecipherable]

These blacks seem [gentle?] & gave me a rabbit they had
just caught so I gave them my remaining blanket &
[indecipherable] one old fellow took a fancy to my hat,
which was falling to pieces, so I gave it him & have tied my
head in a green mosquito net. [indecipherable] out the
Camel pad to [find?] young men & told them they could
have all they could

find (it is nothing but Corned beef) & the bucket

They seemed to understand a good deal & I tried them to
send a message by smoke signals to Alice Spgs but could not
get that thro' their heads. If they return I will try again. I
sketched a man & his wife & showed them (it is in the
[book?] may do for the [indecipherable] they wanted
[indecipherable] sketched the wo[man?] down & an emu

they reckognised [indecipherable] Kanga all right
[indecipherable] explain that the[indecipherable] that came
up the [indecipherable] & a kangaroo but [don't know?] if
they caught on.

The black returned at d[usk?] with a bag of dried apples
that had evidently been discarded by the raiders & 2 tins of
Corned beef. I mimed that I gave him the beef and walked
24 miles and played the game fairly. I also

gave his lubra the checkered blanket as it was too heavy for me to carry & used at this time of year

blackfellow wears white bands in his hair & has a white haired child so anyone may know him.

Im now going to try the 80 miles dash to Mt [Olga?] will travel allow [indecipherable] is [nearly?]full

Till we [indecipherable] all be well with

Harry

Sandhills | cutting out

Limestone | country

Scale 1————1 = 1 mile (estimated on plans)

punifek | Mr Rennie Bearing
| N 8VV

| Mulga
Sc d | mallee getting dense

Can go | back now

Area | li n b x d ground
| fire
| les
| gges llow

9

All that was left of the last mud-map in Lasseter' Diary.

This is cruel to die of starvation. heartless of all who know I am out here when I didn't return by Xmas they knew there was something wrong May God forgive them & [indecipherable] them in my last hour no food for 2 days now

[Envelope]
Papers pertaining to the death of H.L.B. Lasseter

Lasseter's Diary as dug up in the cave, 1931.

Rene darling

Don't grieve for me I've done my best & have pegged the reef, not strictly according to law as the blacks pinched my miners right & I don't know the number but I photographed the datum post on the Quartz Blow the post is sticking in a water hole & the photo faces north. I made the run in 5 days but the blacks have a sacred place nearby & will pull the peg up for sure.

I've taken the films & will plant them at Winters glen if I can get there the Blight has got me beat all because Jack Jenkins never put the Argerol in the medicine chest as I requested. he got boracic lotion instead which relieves the smart but does not cure.

Take good care of Bobby, Betty & Joy please, I want Bobby to be a Civil Engineer try & educate him for that.

Darling I do love you so I'm sorry I can't be with you at the last but God's will be done

yours ever x Harry xxx

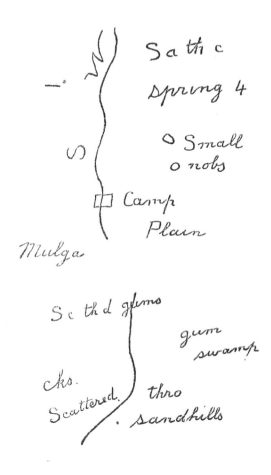

Mud-map from Lasseter's Last Ride, *p245, not in the known diary.*

Mud-map from Lasseter's Last Ride, not in the known diary.

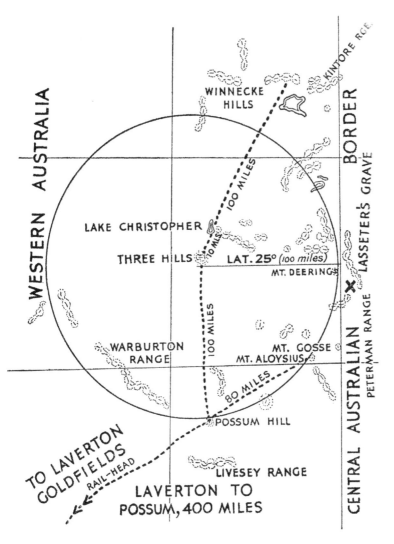

WESTERN AUSTRALIA

BORDER

CENTRAL AUSTRALIAN

KINTORE RGE.

WINNECKE HILLS

LASSETER'S GRAVE

PETERMAN RANGE

LAKE CHRISTOPHER

100 MILES

70 MLS.

THREE HILLS

LAT. 25° (100 miles)

MT. DEERINGS

100 MILES

WARBURTON RANGE

MT. GOSSE
MT. ALOYSIUS

80 MILES

POSSUM HILL

TO LAVERTON GOLDFIELDS

RAIL-HEAD

LIVESEY RANGE

LAVERTON TO POSSUM, 400 MILES

LASSETER'S AREA AND LIVESEY RANGE
The circle shows the area which was held by the C.A.G.E.
Company, Ltd.

Harold Bell Lasseter, 1880 - 1931

Printed in Australia
Ingram Content Group Australia Pty Ltd
AUHW020845160424
393106AU00001B/3